We Go!

Cars

Dana Meachen Rau

Marshall Cavendish
Benchmark
New York

We go in a car.

Cars have hoods.

Cars have lights.

Cars have horns.

Cars have seat belts.

11

Cars carry pets.

13

Cars carry bags.

15

Cars carry bikes.

We go in a car!

19

Words to Know

bags

bikes

hood

horn

lights

pets

seat belt

Index

Page numbers in **boldface** are illustrations.

About the Author

Dana Meachen Rau is the author of many other titles in the Bookworms series, as well as other nonfiction and early reader books. She lives in Burlington, Connecticut, with her husband and two children.

With thanks to the Reading Consultants:

Nanci Vargus, Ed.D., is an Assistant Professor of Elementary Education at the University of Indianapolis.

Beth Walker Gambro is an Adjunct Professor at the University of Saint Francis in Joliet, Illinois.

Marshall Cavendish Benchmark
99 White Plains Road
Tarrytown, New York 10591-9001
www.marshallcavendish.us

Library of Congress Cataloging-in-Publication Data

Rau, Dana Meachen, 1971-
Cars / by Dana Meachen Rau.
p. cm. — (Bookworms. We go!)
Includes index.
Summary: "Describes the physical attributes, different kinds, and purposes of cars"—Provided by publisher.
ISBN 978-0-7614-4078-9
1. Automobiles—Juvenile literature. I. Title.
TL206.R38 2010
629.222—dc22
2008042503

Editor: Christina Gardeski
Publisher: Michelle Bisson
Designer: Virginia Pope
Art Director: Anahid Hamparian

Photo Research by Anne Burns Images

Cover Photo by *Corbis*/Bruce Benedict/Transtock

The photographs in this book are used with permission and through the courtesy of:
Alamy Images: pp. 1, 13, 21BL Juniors Bildarchiv; p. 3 ImageState; pp. 5, 20B Stock Up Images;
pp. 9, 21TL Elvele Images; pp. 11, 21BR Ben Molyneux; pp. 17, 20TR Manor Photography.
SuperStock: pp. 7, 21TR Ron Brown. *Getty Images*: pp. 15, 20TL Paul Taylor; p. 19 Eastphoto.

Printed in Malaysia
1 3 5 6 4 2

10/26/09